English Overseas Trade 1500–1700

Prepared for
the Economic History Society by

RALPH DAVIS

*Professor of Economic History
in the University of Leicester*

MACMILLAN

First published 1973 by
THE MACMILLAN PRESS LTD
London and Basingstoke
Associated companies in New York Toronto
Dublin Melbourne Johannesburg and Madras

SBN 333 14419 8

Printed in Great Britain by
THE ANCHOR PRESS LTD
Tiptree, Essex

Contents

1 *Introduction**

IN the centuries before the Industrial Revolution, English overseas trade went through three waves of expansion, separated by periods of near stagnation. These waves of growth arose out of quite different types of external circumstances, to which English manufacturers and merchants successfully responded and adapted. Between 1475 and 1550 the volume of sales of well-known commodities (broadcloths and some other types of woollen cloth) in long familiar markets of central Europe suddenly began to grow rapidly because these markets were becoming more prosperous. This was not, essentially, the defeating of another industry's competition, nor the widening of the market through cost reductions; incomes expanded rapidly in the existing markets, for reasons that were external to England, and they demanded more of the goods they were accustomed to getting from England. In the second phase, 1630–89, the annual rate of growth was driven forward exceptionally rapidly because there were two expansive elements. One was the capture of south European markets from Italian and Spanish industry, in competition with the Dutch; the decline of the Mediterranean industries that opened these markets to the English and Dutch was an aspect of an overall economic decline whose reasons are disputable, but was, again, external to England. The other expansive element was the creation of virtually new trades, because the cheapness of English-supplied tobacco, sugar and calicoes brought them within the buying capacity of entirely new strata not only of English but also of continental populations. The third phase of trade expansion in the middle decades of the eighteenth century (beyond the scope of this booklet) was derived from the growth of colonial population, production and purchasing power.

* I am grateful to Dr. G. D. Ramsay for reading the draft of this booklet, and producing a host of suggestions which have greatly improved it. I did not always heed his advice, and any errors that remain are therefore wholly my own.

How important was this expanding overseas trade to the English economy and society? The simple gains of inter-country specialisation are obvious enough; it was advantageous to England to produce the woollens in which it still had cost advantages and, in exchange, to forgo the production of linens and wine, so long as the imports could not be substituted for by drawing on unemployed resources. Overseas trade is a very visible phenomenon, producing merchant fortunes, pamphleteering literature, and government intervention and recording; it is easy to over-estimate its significance. It is equally easy to understate it by making mechanical quantiative comparisons. The English, and indeed European, economies were overwhelmingly agricultural throughout these two centuries; as late as 1700, when a considerable shift of national resources away from agriculture had taken place, some two-thirds of employed labour was engaged in agriculture, and a good deal of the remainder was in domestic service of one kind or another. Agricultural improvement provided a very powerful stimulus to the economic progress of the later seventeenth century; but beyond the agricultural sphere, the contribution of overseas trade was of great importance. The reader can do sums for himself, based on Gregory King's estimate of national income for 1688 (though this should be revised upward) and the trade statistics. Simply as food for thought, let me suggest that more than a quarter of all manufacturing production, a half of the production of woollen goods, was exported; that nearly a quarter of home consumption of manufactures was imported, while much of the home production had some significant content of imported materials. These are no more than suggestions as to order of size, attempting to get away from an overall comparison between national production of all goods and services and trade that was, to a large extent, in manufactured goods.

Any considered estimate will demonstrate that overseas trade was very important to the woollen industry in 1700, and this was not necessarily less true in 1500. The woollen industry of 1500 could be broadly divided between, on the one hand, a nearly nation-wide production by small local craftsmen serving their village and town markets and never contemplating international or even inter-regional trade in their products; and on the other, several narrowly localised, highly organised groups of specialist producers selling their goods in widely scattered markets. The

8

relative weight of the second of these two in the national economy had been growing in the later middle ages, and it grew more sharply in the sixteenth and above all in the seventeenth century. These regions of specialised production sold a large part of their output to foreign markets in 1500 and even in 1400; indeed, it is conceivable that their early growth owed more to foreign than to home sales. The scale of the demand for their products made possible extended division of labour, concentration on particular qualities around which specialised skills developed, and a sophisticated organisation of relations between the producer and his market through the domestic system of production. Intra-European trade in manufactures was nearly confined to the specialisms, mainly textiles, produced in a few areas; woollens in parts of the Netherlands and England, linens in parts of France and the Netherlands, silks in a few Italian and French towns. However these specialist industries first arose, their competitive advantages in international markets were reinforced when their great scale enabled them to improve their technical or organisational efficiency. Though there was a modest growth of exports of some other manufactured goods, especially metalwares, after the Civil War, only woollens derived substantial benefits of scale from overseas sales before the eighteenth century.

The expansion of trade created industrial and commercial occupations for its own support—merchants, seamen and warehousemen, shipbuilders, porters and sailmakers, clerks and carters. The growth in employment of labour and capital is not adequately indicated by statistics of the value of trade, for the physical characteristics of trade were changing. Most trade until about 1580 was carried on over short distances, between London and Antwerp or Hamburg. Goods were in transit only for a very short period; stocks were easily replenished and a small merchant fleet could carry them (especially as much of the bulkier raw material import came in Hanseatic or Dutch ships). The resources of labour and capital employed in the service of trade were, therefore, small. During the seventeenth century, while the value of overseas trade rose fivefold, the labour involved in handling it, and the capital necessarily employed, increased far more. Goods were carried over longer distances; the time of transit between London and Cadiz, Danzig, Barbados or Surat was much longer than between London and Antwerp. Moreover, in the distant and loosely organised harbours, with more uncertain market hinterlands, to which traders increasingly penetrated, the discharge of outward cargoes, the mustering of returns, and the collection of debts took far longer than it did in the great ports of Europe. The merchant therefore had to provide finance for very long periods—a year or more in American or eastern Mediterranean trades—between his purchase of goods for export and the sale of his returns at the end. If this caused him to demand and receive increasingly long credit from English manufacturers (and this seems to be a feature of the seventeenth century), he had to give corresponding credit on the goods he sold in England. He had to establish agency houses in foreign ports and, in some trades, found it desirable to extend long credit to the producers of the goods he wished to buy. Moreover, while before 1660 most long voyages had brought back goods of high value per ton, such as silk from Turkey or pepper and calicoes from India, by 1700 the tonnage of long distance cargoes was made up largely of the relatively cheap American tobacco and sugar. The number and tonnage of ships employed in overseas trade rose more rapidly than its value, and at home a correspondingly greater force of warehousemen, porters and carters was needed to shift the goods.

The investment of merchants' resources in the finance of stocks of goods making these long transits, and in the ships needed to carry them, was therefore greatly multiplied. It is unlikely that the value of overseas trade rose faster than national income in the sixteenth century. In the seventeenth century the value of trade evidently grew much more rapidly than national income; and resources of capital and labour employed to carry on trade rose faster still. This accounts for the concentration on problems of trade seen in the seventeenth century writings on economic affairs. By 1700 ships and porterage occupied a very important section of the urban labour force, especially in London; overseas trade supplied goods that went into nearly every household and sold the products of an important part of the nation. Finally, it was the most common path to great wealth for individuals, and provided examples to encourage ambition and enterprise.

2 The Old Trades

ENGLISH exports grew rapidly from the end of the 1470s until the end of Henry VII's reign, though interrupted briefly at times of international tensions. After 1508–10 progress slackened, and though London's trade showed a continuing rapid expansion, this resulted from diversion of much of the trade of the southern and western ports to the metropolis. In the forties and early fifties there were violent trade fluctuations. Exports were very high in some individual years. They collapsed in 1542–3 and 1547 when war cut Antwerp from its continental markets, but surged forward in the intervening and following years. The heavy currency devaluation of 1546 stimulated them to reach a high peak in 1548–50. The epidemic of 1551, the upward revaluation of the currency in 1551–2 and the quarrel with Hanseatic traders in 1552–3 drove them down again. London exports fell away slightly from the highest peaks of the mid-century, but there was compensation, to an extent that cannot be evaluated, in the recovery of exports through the provincial ports. There were individual years of extreme difficulty, as in 1563 and 1586. Heroic efforts had to be made to open new channels of trade as old ones closed and London lost a part of its trading dominance; but English exports probably showed a modest rising tendency during the second half of the century. (16ᵗʰ C)

Until the late seventeenth century, English export trade rested on wool and woollen cloth. The once great export of wool finally collapsed to insignificance in 1521. Other commodities, such as tin, lead, skins and fish, were sent out only in very small quantities. Cloth, therefore, provides a reasonable measure of the development of export trade. The total quantity of cloth exported was more than doubled between the mid-1470s and the peak years around 1550, and, in this period of rising prices, the value must have risen even more.[1] From the second decade of the sixteenth

[1] For London and provincial ports exports of cloth, 1473–1561, see Table I, page 52 below.

century, there emerged a striking concentration of trade on London at the expense of provincial ports—the substitution, indeed, of an intensive traffic between London and the single continental market of Antwerp, for a widely distributed trade embracing many English and continental ports. Trade with Spain, carried on from Southampton and Bristol as well as from London, made a contribution to the early phase of expansion, but it fell away after 1520. For some decades, Spanish merchants did much of their business with England through the Antwerp intermediary, though the importance of such bulky goods as wine and iron in cargoes from Spain prevented the direct trade from dying out completely. The direct seaborne trade with Italy, based on Southampton, in which Italians had been joined by English merchants late in the fifteenth century, grew very fast until after 1520, but then collapsed as the growing dangers from Moorish piracy in the Western Mediterranean encouraged a resort to the overland route through Antwerp to Italy. From the 1520s the whole trade of southern and western ports, which was directed to southern Europe, was in serious decline; even the French trade weakened as the demand for one of its chief return commodities, Toulouse woad, went out of use. By mid-century, the only provincial port that retained an important trade was Hull, which sent substantial quantities of Yorkshire kerseys and dozens in Hanseatic ships to ports of the North Sea and the Baltic. In 1500 London had accounted for less than half of England's cloth exports; in some years of the 1540s its share approached nine-tenths.

The growth of English trade, and its concentration on the London–Antwerp connection, was associated with the increasing wealth of the German lands of central Europe, and of markets further east served by German traders. In the second half of the fifteenth century the extraction and refining of minerals—copper, lead, zinc and, above all, silver—had been developed on an unprecedented scale in the mountainous regions of the Bohemian, Moravian and Hungarian borderlands. Towns and industries grew up serving the prosperous mining communities, and a great thriving area in southern Germany and lands to the east exported its metals and metal wares in return for the manufactures and materials of the Middle East and Italy on the one side, and of the Netherlands and England on the other. English cloth was already well-known and popular in central European mar-

12

kets. In the early fifteenth century it had had some difficulty in
getting access to them, for the great medieval port of Bruges clung
to its role as the outlet of the Flemish woollen industry, and would
not handle English cloths that competed with it. The English
merchants, after prospecting among a number of the towns of
the Rhine-Scheldt delta, had finally settled, in the 1440s, on Antwerp, which had a useful trading affiliation with Cologne. In the
last quarter of the century, when Antwerp received an enormous
stimulus from rising central European incomes, traders in
English cloth shared the benefits. Around Antwerp's central acti-
vity of trade, between England and the northern Netherlands
on the one hand, and Cologne and the German towns to the
east on the other, the city rapidly built up a role as the natural
place of exchange for all kinds of goods that came or went across
Europe and that, at some point, touched the North Sea coast.
Portuguese traders settled in Antwerp, buying German copper
wares for the African trade from the 1470s, and silver for India
after 1504; in return they sold sugar and spices from the Atlantic
islands and the Indian Ocean. After 1459 Italian vessels called
at Antwerp as well as Bruges. In the early sixteenth century Rouen
merchants bought their Mediterranean and Spanish goods at
Antwerp in exchange for Normandy linens; and the German
and Dutch traders who carried timber, flax and corn into Antwerp's Dutch satellite towns spent much of the proceeds on purchases to send back from Antwerp. Early sixteenth century Antwerp was a meeting place for merchants of all nations—English,
German, Flemish, Italian, Spanish, French, Portuguese; even
Syrians and Greeks and an occasional Hindu. A merchant could
rely on finding goods from most parts of Europe and much of
the world, and above all on a wide choice of the luxury manufactures of the English, Dutch, French and Italian textile industries. Moreover, the exchange facilities were good, so that it was
not essential to return goods for goods; remittances could be
made to or from the chief centres of Europe by bills of exchange.
Antwerp became the great entrepôt of north-west Europe, drawing many branches of trade away from direct routes between
producing and consuming centres, and the concentration of English trade on London in the first half of the sixteenth century was
simply one very important consequence of Antwerp's drawing
power.

13

The particular products that central Europe absorbed in great quantities were heavy broadcloths manufactured in Gloucester, Wiltshire, and eastern Somerset, which were sent through London in an unfinished state to Antwerp, and dyed and finished there to meet the precise standards of their continental markets. London owed its new trading importance, initially, to its favourable geographical situation for handling goods going from Gloucester and Wiltshire to Antwerp; its merchants cemented their hold on the Antwerp trade, at the beginning of the sixteenth century, by securing the crown's acquiescence in their control over the Company of Merchants Adventurers to which all Englishmen trading with the Low Countries had to belong.

Yet much of English—and even of London—trade was of a different kind. The goods sent to Antwerp for onward carriage by overland routes to Italy were not broadcloths but kerseys. Even the best kerseys manufactured in Hampshire and Berkshire, that were used in this trade, were much lighter and cheaper than broadcloths, and English dyeing and finishing were adequate for most of them. This through traffic to Italy, and beyond it into the Balkans and east Europe through Venice and Ragusa, accounted for much of the growth of London's Antwerp trade in the second quarter of the sixteenth century. In two short periods (1535) and (1551) in which transits of cloth through Antwerp are recorded, the number of kerseys was not much smaller than that of broadcloths, though their total value was a great deal less. Even the broadcloths going through London included many dyed Suffolk and Kent cloths destined for ultimate sale in the German and Swedish coastal areas of the Baltic; and the cheap northern kerseys that went from Newcastle and Hull—increasingly through Antwerp—to the Baltic, were all dyed and finished in their Yorkshire producing area. It is doubtful whether, even at their mid-century peak, the export of undyed and undressed cloths accounted for more than half of English cloth exports in value.

In the three decades that followed the mid-century boom, the English connection with Antwerp was first weakened and then completely broken. Antwerp's extraordinary entrepôt position was coming under pressure before mid-century, no more than thirty years after it had reached its apogee. From the 1530s, a little English cloth was being finished at Hamburg rather than

Antwerp; in the 1540s, the Portuguese were buying German copper at Venice, and silver at Seville instead of Antwerp. The mineral-based prosperity of central Europe began to fail as American silver arrived in quantity. The long wars in central Europe between 1545 and 1555 repeatedly obstructed the routes of trade and brought ruin to trading cities; and the bankruptcies of the French and the Spanish crowns in 1557, arising out of the costs of these wars, dealt a cruel shock to the Antwerp money market. But the slow changes that were beginning to reduce the range of Antwerp's activities were overtaken by political events that directed a series of strong and soon fatal blows straight at Antwerp itself and, in different fashion, at the English connection with it. From the nationalist and religious quarrels in Europe stemmed the Netherlands struggle for independence that began in 1568 and broke out into open war against Spain in 1572. After 1572 Antwerp's commercial attractions faded rapidly; the sack of the city by mutinous Spanish troops in 1576 ruined many merchants and drove others away, and those who lingered witnessed the final strangling of Antwerp's seaborne trade when in 1585 the Dutch were able to close the Scheldt to traffic and so cut Antwerp off from the sea. Meanwhile, the spread of Protestantism rapidly worsened English relations with the Spanish rulers of the Low Countries; growing suspicion and latent hostility between Elizabethan England and Spain built up an atmosphere in which small incidents led to serious quarrels. Trading relations were twice broken off between the territories of the Spanish crown (including Antwerp) and England : in 1563–4, on pretexts of danger from the plague and English piracy in the Channel, and again in 1568–73, in consequence of disputes that arose from Channel privateering. These two Anglo-Spanish quarrels pre-dated the serious decline of Antwerp's own trading position, but the temporary absences of English traders encouraged and hastened the more general exodus of merchants and trade.

The breaches with Antwerp posed very serious problems for the merchants who carried on English trade. Concentration on Antwerp had caused old trading links with many other parts of Europe to be broken, and one of the hardest things to re-establish was confident relations with merchants across the seas. Even if new trading connections were established, the greatest market still demanded cloth dyed and finished to Antwerp's standards, which English clothworkers could not meet. Finally, if some kinds of English-finished cloth could be sent directly to Baltic and Mediterranean ports, the problem emerged of processing goods that had to be brought back in return—for London lacked Antwerp's processing industries—or of re-exporting surpluses of them beyond England's own needs.

There was a ready geographical substitute for the Rhine route that led into Germany by Antwerp and Cologne; this was the Elbe route through Hamburg, the main inland centre of which was Leipzig. The English traders who were suddenly excluded from the Netherlands in 1563 hurriedly made arrangements to trade at Emden, conveniently situated just across the Netherlands border. But it was a small market, which attracted few Italian or German merchants, and English cloth exports dropped sharply in 1563–4. Once the immediate quarrel had been patched up and trade through Antwerp resumed, London merchants insured against the recurrence of such a setback by entering into negotiations with Hamburg, securing in 1567 a ten-year agreement giving them an assured right to trade there with minor privileges. This enabled them to get through the breach of relations with Antwerp after 1568 without great difficulty. Between 1568 and 1573 an enormous cloth trade was carried on through Hamburg, great quantities were dyed and finished in the city, and it appeared for a time that Hamburg might be built up by the English connection in the same way as Antwerp. But England had been quarrelling with the Hanseatic League for a quarter of a century over the reduction of Hanse privileges in England, and England's new dependence on entry to Europe through Germany gave the Hanse an opportunity to exert pressure to get its own way. Hamburg was forced to expel the English after their agreement expired in 1577, though many lingered for two or three years. Nevertheless, Hamburg had carried English trade through the period of greatest upheaval and uncertainty in the Netherlands. By the early 1580s the Dutch part of the Netherlands was beginning to appear temporarily secure, and those English traders who had persisted at Antwerp until its last days were able to establish a new settlement in Dutch territory at Middelburg in 1582. In Germany, Emden was again the principal English settlement from 1579 to 1587, but in the latter year the small town of Stade, just

16

beyond the Hamburg city limits, was adopted as staple town for the trade, and the fact that English cloth dyeing at Hamburg reached a new peak in 1587–8 indicates that Stade was simply a stepping-stone to dealings at the greater centre.

The rapid export expansion of the early Tudor period was not resumed after the final mid-century peak. The raw figures of London woollen exports between 1555 and 1604, it is true, give an unduly pessimistic impression. After 1558 customs statistics regularly understate the numbers exported by one-ninth, because of the institution of a rule that allowed one cloth in ten to go free of duty as a wrapper. Moreover, the worsteds that went out in increasing quantities from the 1570s are not included in the statistics. Even so, London's total exports probably remained a little below the average of the decade 1545–54; but, on the other hand, the extreme concentration of England's trade on London, which had characterised those years, was brought to an end. There was an expansion of direct trade, from London and provincial ports, with parts of Europe that had for fifty years or more been dealt with mainly through the intermediary of Antwerp. The limiting factor in this response to new conditions was the possibility of extending the markets that would take English-finished cloths—which meant, on the whole, not broadcloths but cheaper and coarser types.[2]

There had already been new stirrings in the ports of the north-east and south-west coasts. The continuing need in northern England for flax, pitch and tar—cheap goods that were needed to minimise transport costs—had ensured the continuance of a direct connection with the Baltic. As early as the 1540s, the direct traffic of Hull and York with the Baltic was beginning to expand a little. In the following decades the number of ships in this traffic grew rapidly, and between 1565 and 1585 the number of northern kerseys and dozens that passed through the Sound into the Baltic increased sixfold. These were Yorkshire cloths going mainly from York and Hull, but London merchants had a share in the trade as well. Danzig was the focus of trade with the Baltic, and its trading relations with England became more active after the Antwerp crisis of 1568. But here, too, the Anglo-Hanse quarrel made

[2] For cloth and certain other exports from London, 1598–1669, see Table II, page 53 below.

17

its influence felt in the seventies, and an alternative Baltic centre had to be found. In 1579 the small town of Elbing defied the crumbling powers of the Hanseatic League by offering privileges to English traders, and these were taken up by London as well as by provincial merchants, who came together to form the Eastland Company. Baltic trade through Elbing expanded to reach a peak in the 1590s, when huge imports of corn to relieve the English harvest failures of 1594–6 paid for Baltic purchases of kerseys, dozens and Suffolk broadcloths in quantities that made a substantial contribution to the total of English trade. The new manufacture of Devon and Dorset friezes, which began to find a French market in the 1530s, expanded it greatly after the mid-century; a little later, Chester was building an export of Welsh cloths to France, and all these goods were sold in smaller quantities in Spain and Portugal. The successful exploitation by provincial merchants of these newly enlarged trades in cheaper and, above all, finished cloths, which was assisted from 1572 onward by wars that ravaged the Flemish centres of manufacture of light worsteds, presently attracted the participation of the Londoners who encountered difficulties in their traditional markets.

As for trade with countries to the south, the south-east European markets supplied by Italy bought types of cloth that were normally finished in England—Hampshire, Kent and Berkshire kerseys. Indeed, before Antwerp's final closure, there had been some resumption of the trade with Italy by sea. The number of Venetian ships coming to England showed some revival in the 1560s. The Spanish embargo on trade with England in 1569–73, and the temporary cessation of the Venetians' visits when they were engaged in war with the Turks, 1570–3, caused English merchants to send their ships into the Mediterranean, selling English cloth and bring back olive oil from southern Italy and currants from the Ionian Islands. They were encouraged to establish factors at Leghorn, which the Duke of Tuscany was trying to turn into a major port, and were inevitably attracted to Venice. The final step in establishing trade throughout the Mediterranean was the negotiation of trading rights in the Turkish Empire, and in 1581 London merchants founded the Levant Company to carry on trade with Turkey, Syria and Egypt. In consequence of all this the great overland trade in kerseys, that had supplied the Balkans, Turkey and even Persia through Ant-

18

werp in the middle decades of the century, reverted to sea routes that took them to Venice, Spalato, Ragusa and Constantinople.

The drive into the Baltic, and especially into the Mediterranean, was by no means solely motivated by the desire to sell English cloth. Antwerp and the Dutch ports had supplied England with many of the goods of northern and southern Europe, and means had to be found to obtain them when the Netherlands market was disrupted. The Dutch carriage of corn, hemp, flax and tar fell to a low level in the 1570s and 1580s, and England was driven to supply itself directly from the Baltic or northern Russia. The market for Mediterranean and Asian produce at Antwerp was constantly interrupted by war, and olive oil and dyestuffs for the English textile industry, as well as minor luxuries like dried fruits, spices and sugar, had to be sought in places further afield. Indeed, even earlier than this, it seems probable that the dangers that appeared in carrying on Mediterranean trade after the Turks exerted their maritime strength in the central Mediterranean account not only for English withdrawal from the trade for several decades, but also for some of the extra European ventures of English traders. The occasional Brazilian and West African voyages of the 1530s and 1540s, the more regular Morocco trade that grew out of them, and even John Hawkins' ventures into the Caribbean in the 1560s, sought goods that England had obtained from the Mediterranean lands. New attempts to find a direct route to Asia, however, had a more political motivation, in the desire of the extremist Protestant government under Edward VI to secure Asian goods independently of Spain or Portugal. For this purpose the aged Spanish pilot-major, Sebastian Cabot, was brought to England as an adviser to the crown in 1547, and the unexpected result of the expeditions initiated under his guidance was the establishment of trade with northern Russia (by the White Sea) through which came, from time to time, Persian silk and Indian spices.

X 3 *The Opening of Southern Trades*

THE markets into which English cloth exports flowed in increasing quantity from the fifteenth century onward were on the whole those of the central and north European lands south of the North Sea and Baltic, and north of the Alps and Pyrenees. In this area they competed with great success against the older Flemish industry in a range of fine and coarse woollen cloths, and, during the later fifteenth century, Flanders adapted itself to this situation by transferring its efforts to lighter, generally worsted cloths. Central European prosperity, a change of fashion among the well-to-do that substituted heavy cloth for furs, and the final triumph over Flemish competition, all contributed to the rapid rise of English exports in the last quarter of the fifteenth century. But southern European markets were almost untouched by English products, beyond modest sales in Spain in exchange for wine and oil. The kerseys that went to Italy were finally sold in the Turkish Balkans, Hungary and Asia Minor (which could not be approached across their German frontiers) rather than in the main Mediterranean markets. Powerful and well-established industries in Italy and Catalonia, and a growing Castilian woollen industry, with ample supplies of Spanish wool, met most of the needs of the countries round the Mediterranean, and only the new Flemish worsteds penetrated their markets at all seriously in the first three-quarters of the sixteenth century.

The rising tide of English cloth exports going into central Europe reached a high water mark early in the sixteenth century; continuing expansion of trade through Antwerp was largely attributable to the transit trade to Italy. The central European trade retained its absolute importance—though the composition of the export changed in later years—but other branches of trade grew up alongside and eventually outstripped it. In Scandinavia and the Baltic, the troubles of Netherlands industry and trade after 1572 left a vacuum in which English exports filled a place; after the 1590s this trade receded, but it was recovered again rapidly

in the later seventeenth century as growing west European demands for Baltic products increased the purchasing power of the
area. This northern trade, however, made only a modest contribution to the total of exports. The great seventeenth century
development took place in new markets to the south. English
manufactures, which had been seen only in small quantities south
of the Alps and Pyrenees, suddenly found a huge market in Spain,
presently supplemented this in Portugal and Italy, and expanded
their sale in these areas almost continuously until they reached
saturation after the middle of the eighteenth century. There are
difficulties in expressing this statistically, but it is probable that
in the 1530s more than four-fifths of English cloth exports were
destined for central and north European markets, in the early
years of the seventeenth century certainly as much as nine-tenths,
by 1640 no more than two-thirds, and by 1700 only a half.[3]

Exploratory feelers towards the south were made by Devon
traders, who may have seen opportunities of selling their light
cloths when the Flemish industry's troubles began, and by London
merchants seeking an alternative market with the aid of the East
Anglian 'New Draperies' when their Antwerp trade was obstructed. But their early successes were modest, for the Mediterranean textile industries were still vigorous. The great opportunities arose after 1600 from changing relationships between the
conditions of production in English, Mediterranean, and Low
Countries cloth industries.

The decline in Italian and Spanish industry became obvious
from the 1620s. The reasons for the Italian and Spanish collapse
that left their markets open are far from clear; but it was by no
means confined to textiles, and cannot, therefore, be wholly attri-
buted to a new efficiency in English competition. If their wool
supply became inadequate or over-expensive, this was largely because the Netherlands and England were willing to outbid Spanish
or Italian producers to buy it. The heavy fall of population in
Spain between 1594 and 1611 appears to have created labour
shortages that pushed some wages up sharply, and the re-
curring population losses in Mediterranean countries and France,
that were not experienced in England or the Netherlands, may

[3] For exports of Old Draperies to northern and southern Europe,
early seventeenth century, see Table III, page 54 below.

have tended to keep wages high. Rising wages and the rigidity of gild-encrusted industries, particularly in the Spanish towns, pushed costs upward during a period when English wages were notoriously unresponsive to the rise in living costs. There was a sharp weakening of the whole Mediterranean economy, for reasons that its historians are still disputing, and although this reduced purchasing power in the area, the transfer of even a lessened demand for woollens from southern to northern industry gave the latter an enormously enlarged market. It included, moreover, the Spanish and Portuguese colonies whose trade was channelled through Seville and Lisbon. Whatever the causes of the Mediterranean decline, its result was that the competitive struggle, during the middle decades of the seventeenth century about the market shares of English and Low Countries industries for particular kinds of cloth, was especially directed at these freshly opening markets of the south. The French and, rather later, German woollen industries were growing sporadically, capturing a part of their home markets with the aid, eventually, of some state protection; but neither was a very substantial exporter before the end of the seventeenth century. Through the last three-quarters of the seventeenth century, the rivals in woollen exporting were England and the Netherlands.

England's penetration of south European markets was made, not by any of its old and famous types of woollen cloth, but by the new woollen (or, strictly, worsted and semi-worsted) products that were being made in England from the 1560s onward under the general title of the 'New Draperies'.

The manufacture of varieties of worsteds—that is, cloths made with combed long-staple wool and not fulled (as distinct from what are technically called woollens, made from carded short-staple wool and fulled so as to obscure the pattern)—was carried on in many parts of Europe. It had long been an important part of the Italian and Spanish manufacture that used Spanish wool, and had occupied minor sections of Flemish industry using local wools. As English competition overcame the old fine cloth industry of Flanders in the later middle ages, these lesser branches of Flemish industry improved their products and widened their markets, importing Spanish wool as local supplies ceased to be adequate. Worsteds became the main product of Netherlands industry, which flourished on this new basis during the first two-thirds of the sixteenth century. But from the end of the 1560s until after 1590 the industrial areas were ravaged by the spreading disturbances and the war of independence, and a period of recovery in the first quarter of the next century was succeeded by another bad setback in the Franco-Spanish wars of the 1630s and 1640s.

The most powerful influence towards rapid development of the worsted manufacture in England (where contemporaries called it the 'New Drapery') was the immigration, in the 1560s, of large numbers of religious refugees from the Netherlands. Among them were textile craftsmen, who brought the Flemish skills of worsted-making to Kent and East Anglia where they settled. But other factors were already at work. The small and moribund Norwich worsted industry was already stirring a little before the refugees arrived, as the continental example created some demand for worsteds in England. The improved type of spinning wheel known as the Saxony wheel, introduced to England in the 1530s, was more suited to the combed wool used for worsted than to short, carded wool. It has been powerfully argued that changing conditions in sheep rearing in sixteenth century England—the increased use of enclosed land on which heavier sheep were bred —was causing a shortage of the short fine wool used for the old types of cloth; that the expansion of New Draperies was to some extent a consequence of the increasing supply of long, coarse wool suited to worsted. This conclusion has been disputed, and the balance of the argument is not yet completely clear.

This industry, established in England in the 1560s, grew to an efficient scale on the basis of a home market avid for its products, for the early development of its export market was cut off by the Anglo-Spanish war. It eventually achieved large export sales when Mediterranean industries were collapsing, and particularly in the 1630s when the Dutch who had been exploiting this situation were heavily involved in war. Once firmly established in Mediterranean markets, the English industry began to pull ahead of its Dutch competitors, and hardly paused in its expansion for well over a century.

Despite the appearance of the New Draperies, and the widening of the geographical sphere into which English goods penetrated directly, the export of broadcloths through London to a mart town in Holland or Germany settled on by the Merchants

23

Adventurers, for ultimate sale in central Europe, remained the largest branch of trade until after the Civil War. It flourished in the period of fairly general peace between 1604 and 1614, attaining a final peak in the three years after English traders were readmitted to Hamburg in 1611. In these years London again sent two-thirds of its cloth exports to the Dutch and German mart towns and four-fifths of these were unfinished broadcloths. Nevertheless, the complete dominance of London over English trade had long since passed away; even in these successful years less than two-thirds of all England's exports passed through it. The Hull–Baltic trade in northern kerseys and dozens, the trade carried on from a string of ports between Weymouth and Plymouth in sending Devon and Dorset dozens to France, and Chester export of Welsh cloth to France, had all been built up to high levels during Elizabeth's reign, and the southern trade in which provincial ports had a share was already significant.

At much the same time, the Dutch cloth industry, centred on Leyden, began to compete successfully with London's basic export of heavy broadcloth. Contemporaries believed that English superiority in this manufacture depended on the monopoly of high-quality wool, and that Dutch competition was made possible by the improvement of Spanish wool. A stimulus was given to Dutch competitors by the English government's prohibition in 1615 of the export of undyed and undressed cloth, in an attempt to force the sale of English-finished cloth on the continent. This, the Cockayne affair, disorganised the broadcloth trade for three years, and it was claimed that it gave the Dutch industry its foothold among England's customers. But while the fall of the broadcloth export began in this way, it continued throughout the century. There was a particularly serious drop in sales in the early twenties, when much of the continental market was thrown into confusion by the beginning of the Thirty Years' War (1618–48); and again in the forties when the English Civil War disrupted communications between London and the main producing areas. The most powerful long-run influence, however, was the change in fashion away from the wearing of these very heavy cloths. The market that the Dutch were successfully penetrating was a declining one.

Though the Cockayne experiment was organised to benefit royal favourites, it was not altogether absurd. An effort to stimulate the carrying out of dyeing and finishing processes in England was reasonable enough; indeed, it is remarkable that the disappearance of Antwerp's facilities had not long since resulted in the development of dyeing in England. Refugees had come over with skill in dyeing, dyestuffs were imported from Holland and the Mediterranean, and in wartime great quantities of dyewoods and cochineal were taken in Spanish ships by privateers. Dyeing of cloth in Gloucestershire did, apparently, begin to make some progress after 1609, and the Cockayne project, premature by only a few years, may have gained plausibility from knowledge of this. New Turkish and Indian markets for broadcloths, first tested with Suffolk cloth in the 1590s, were exploited more thoroughly as western broadcloth dyed in London became available in the 1620s and 1630s, and they helped the industry to survive the decline in its older markets.

The English cloth industry was running with a fashionable tide in turning over to worsted. All over western and central Europe men and women showed willingness to welcome the new clothing materials, and while Yorkshire kerseys and dozens remained popular in northern Europe, the friezes, Devon dozens and the like were going out of favour even more rapidly than broadcloths from the 1630s onward. The search for variety led not only to new woollens and worsteds and mixed fabrics—serges, camlets, bays, moccadoes, perpetuanas, says, rashes and so on—but to a growing use of cottons and linens, and, among the more prosperous people, of silks and velvets. In the first half of the seventeenth century old sections of the woollen industry were going down before the advance of new ones; but towards its end, those new ones were to be seriously menaced by cheap oriental textiles.

4 England as Importer

MERCHANTS traded in order to make profits, and they did so by either importing or exporting, or more commonly by a combination of both. It would be wrong to suppose that penetration to new trading areas was always a search for new markets; commonly its purpose was more direct access to the sources of imported foodstuffs or materials. Indeed, the best opportunities for securing more than routine gains from trade were usually to be found in importing. Most exported cloth was sold in great international markets (especially in the sixteenth and the early seventeenth century), where there was a concourse of buyers and sellers. There was competition not only between English and foreign merchants who sent out English cloth, but also with foreigners selling foreign cloth; and the buyers were usually large wholesale merchants with resources and skills at least equal to those of the exporters. There were many wealthy traders on both sides, whose capacity to hold stocks evened out price fluctuation. Though imported goods were sold in England under competitive conditions, the merchants faced much weaker and less well-informed buyers. Mercery wares were often sold retail, or to small chapmen stocking up their packs to carry through the countryside, or to modest merchant intermediaries who took them round the fairs. Wines, spices, fruit and sugar were exotic products, more or less perishable, whose prices fluctuated wildly according to supply expectations. The principal motive of extra-European exploration and trading enterprise, from 1547 onward, was to tap the original sources of supply of the more exotic foodstuffs and materials, above all in Asia; the early English explorations in North America were intended to find a western route to Asia. Asia was known to provide only a poor market for European goods and its produce had to be paid for largely in bullion. Yet the trade was highly desirable because of the commodities it offered; it was lack of knowledge of the routes, and political obstacles, rather than absence of desire to trade, that

26

held back the north-west European nations from Asia until the very end of the sixteenth century. The chief English imports in the sixteenth century were mostly luxuries, headed by wine. In 1500 wine—coming almost entirely from the French ports of Bordeaux and Rochelle—may still have accounted for nearly half of England's imports. This must have been a difficult trade to sustain, for France was not a large importer of English wares, and most of them went into Norman and Breton ports rather than to Gascony. Some Rhenish wine was imported, and a slowly growing quantity of Spanish wines from Malaga and Cadiz and the Canary Islands. As English exports to Spain grew rapidly through the middle decades of the seventeenth century, so did the import of Spanish wine, which found favour in a consuming taste which was more concerned with the strength than with any other qualities. Beyond this, most sixteenth century imports were manufactures, bought in Antwerp although their places of origin were various. They were probably headed by Italian silks and velvets, but included quantities of linens, handkerchiefs, scarves and stockings made in the Low Countries, German fustians, many kinds of metal goods from Liège and from Germany, and other items such as gloves, paper and glassware. The variety was endless, with much of the value embodied in small luxury articles for the rich that provided the counterpart of the English export trade through Antwerp. There were necessary imports such as dyestuffs for the woollen industry, and salt, iron and hemp, as well as sugar, currants, spices and other table delicacies, but their total value was not large. Wine remained a stable element in English import trade, but its relative weight in the total declined rapidly. English industrial development from the latter part of the sixteenth century changed the character of the import trade in manufactures. The import of bays, says and moccadoes from Antwerp was replaced by the English manufacture of the New Draperies. The making of many iron, copper and brass wares, as well as coarse paper, glass and salt—largely under the impulses of expanded mineral extraction and refining in England—reduced dependence on many minor imports. On the other hand, the import of linens expanded rapidly, for there was a rising English demand as the use of linen spread down the social scale. But the big changes in imports were associated with the widening of the geographical bounds of Eng-

27

lish trade. Necessity drove England to import much more from the Baltic and Scandinavian lands, increased imports from the south resulted from the expansion of exports and the new trading connections they involved, and the warm lands beyond Europe offered imports that were not necessary, but attractive in terms of merchant profit and consumer satisfaction.[4]

Trade with the Baltic and Scandinavian countries was always complicated by their specially close relationship with the Dutch ports and Antwerp. During the sixteenth century, when Antwerp handled the most valuable commodities of international trade (textiles, metalwares and spices), its merchants also helped to finance the trade of Amsterdam and other Dutch ports in cheap bulky commodities from the north (corn, timber, flax, hemp, tar and pitch), and the return of salt, herrings and wine. Competition for carrying and selling these cargoes was carried on between Dutch and Hanseatic traders; the English were at a disadvantage, for they needed only small amounts of the main Baltic cargoes, timber and corn. As the scale of the Dutch carrying trade expanded, they were able to develop specialised types of ships for Baltic commodities that gave them real advantages in efficiency over their rivals. During the sixteenth century, therefore, the Dutch share of Baltic trade was growing; their towns became entrepôts for Baltic goods, where merchants knew they could readily obtain quantities and assortments of timber, corn at all times of the year, hemp, flax, tallow and other things, and get them shipped without delay to their destinations. This entrepôt position, badly dented during some years of the 1570s and 1580s when the most intense phase of the struggle against Spain engaged almost all Dutch effort, was rapidly recovered in the last years of the century. The resources that supported it were enhanced by the concentration of refugee wealth and talent from southern Flanders in Amsterdam, so that during the first half of the next century, the Dutch Republic was unquestionably the great commercial power of Europe.

The direct English trade with the Baltic, that expanded during the period of Dutch difficulties and the years of big English corn imports in the 1590s, fell away rapidly in the early seven-

[4] For London imports 1621, 1660, 1700, see Table IV, page 55 below.

28

teenth century. A growing share of imports of northern goods was bought at the Dltch entrepôt, and there was a striking increase in the export from Hull and London to Holland of cloth that was obviously intended for Baltic destinations. England's need for northern goods grew rapidly in the seventeenth century, though its character changed. The import of Baltic corn, though not again reaching the level of particular years in the mid-1590s, came to be more regular during the first half of the new century, though it ended abruptly in 1650. The need for imports to meet intermittent grain shortages, however, was beginning to be overshadowed by a more permanent requirement for new materials from the Baltic and Scandinavia. Sixteenth century England imported some hemp and flax for ropes and canvas, and small amounts of timber, potash and tar. The quantities were increasing in the last quarter of the century, as English shipping was enlarged to handle a geographically widening trade, and as some of the most accessible home supplies of timber for both house and shipbuilding began to be worked out. In the second quarter of the seventeenth century there was a sharp acceleration in imports of these goods, particularly timber, and, at the same time, a big import of Swedish iron began in consequence of the introduction of modern smelting techniques to the high-quality Swedish ores in the 1620s. Danzig and Königsberg, the old centres of Baltic trade with England, which were markets for English cloth and collecting points for the shipment of corn and flax, were overhauled in importance by the timber loading harbours of the south Norwegian fiords, the iron-shipping centres of Gothenburg and Stockholm, and the north Baltic ports that offered hemp, flax, pitch, tar and mast timber.

As these trades grew in size, English merchants and shipowners pressed their government for assistance against Dutch competition. An Order in Council of 1615 had required the bringing of Mediterranean goods to England only in English ships and a similar order was applied to the Baltic in 1622. The situation was eased by the heavy involvement of the Dutch in the Thirty Years' War, and when this was over a decisive blow was struck at both the Dutch entrepôt trade and the carriage of Baltic goods to England in Dutch ships by the Navigation Act of 1651. The northern trades, still expanding rapidly in value—the value of London's Baltic trade trebled between 1622 and 1669 and con-

29

tinued to grow very fast—became great employers of English merchant resources and, above all, because of their bulk, of English shipping.

For a long time, exports directly paid for these necessary imports, rising when corn imports were large and falling when they were small. From the 1620s, however, there was a rapidly growing deficit on the direct trade, met from the surplus on trade with Holland. Throughout the second half of the century, English importers from the Baltic regularly settled their obligations by drawing bills of exchange on Amsterdam. In the Norwegian timber trade, in which there was a similar import surplus, silver was regularly shipped out for payment, despite its illegality before 1662.

The trades with the southern countries of Europe grew under quite different influences. From the second quarter of the seventeenth century the Iberian peninsula's capacity to absorb great quantities of English goods (for its internal and its American colonial needs) stimulated trade with it in both directions. The export earnings from woollens, that mounted spectacularly from the 1630s, were augmented—probably outstripped—by the proceeds of the enormous quantities of cod caught by English fishermen on the Newfoundland Banks and carried to Spain. Of course, Englishmen were conscious of the great flow of silver that came into Spain each year, but there is no strong reason to suppose that they traded with Spain to secure silver; this spread through Europe and reached England by other channels. The problem of finding a way to pay for growing exports to Spain and Portugal was solved by the expansion of imports, first evidenced by the dramatic leap of the import figures in the 1630s. Rising imports of the familiar wine, wool and oil were supplemented by great amounts of fruit—raisins, figs and oranges—with Portugal supplying wine from Madeira and later from Portugal itself, and Brazil sugar. Expanded cloth exports to Italy in the thirties were similarly met by returns of Italian silk and oil, as well as some Levant goods. The increased traffic by sea with Italy, in both directions, was a renewed and final substitution of seaborne trade for the trans-European trade which, revived after the general peace of 1609, was again wrecked by the Thirty Years' War.

At the other end of the Mediterranean, seaborne trade with the Turkish Empire was reopened in the 1580s, when the old desire

30

for direct access to Asian products was given new strength by the blocking of the routes through Antwerp, by which they had reached England. Early imports from the Levant were mainly of Indian and Indonesian nutmegs, indigo, pepper and drugs, and while some kerseys and tin were exported to pay for them, there was an adverse balance which had to be met by shipping silver. After the Dutch began in 1597 to use the Cape route to the Far East, the English Levant merchants rightly feared that their transit trade would be destroyed, and for this reason they helped to promote the English East India Company to compete with the Dutch in the Indian Ocean itself. But their old trade did not decay, for the Levant itself could provide goods that were increasingly demanded in western Europe—above all, raw silk from Persia, but also galls, cotton, mohair yarn and dyestuffs. Meanwhile the balance of the trade was changing; the decline of the Italian woollen industry, whose effect on Iberian markets has already been noticed, opened the way to English sales of fine woollens in Turkey. Rising exports of broadcloths ended the need to send silver to Turkey after the 1620s, and for half a century the problem of this trade was one of finding imports to pay for exports. It was met by an expansion of the silk trade, and also by developing, as in Spain and Italy, a big trade in raisins, currants and figs. A few of the Mediterranean imports—dyestuffs and oil—were essential to the English woollen industry, and the expansion of Levant trade brought in new raw materials that contributed to the promotion of new industries in England, notably silk and cotton manufactures. Nevertheless, the development of the southern import trades contributed more to the creation and service of new consumer tastes than to industrial growth.

Not till After 1660.

RE-EXPORTS.

5 Trade Beyond Europe

TRADE beyond Continental Europe (except to Mediterranean Turkey) was of little consequence before the Civil War. Then it rose dramatically, to an extent that changed the whole pattern of England's overseas trade. By 1700 America and Asia were providing a third of all imports, and the re-export of their produce accounted for nearly a third of all English exports.[5]

The origins of English trade with Asia and America go back no further than the beginning of the seventeenth century, though preparations and attempts to initiate it were being made long before. All these had stemmed from the desire to take a direct part in the profits of importing Asian goods; to secure the gains that had once made Venice and Genoa, and were now making Lisbon, rich. Direct ways to Asia were sought round the far north and the far south of the American continent and round the north of Asia, before it was finally accepted that the only route was the one the Portuguese had pioneered and now monopolised, round the southern tip of Africa. English merchants were accumulating a formidable body of capital and trading connections, and experience of ocean navigation had grown through West African and Brazilian voyaging around mid-century, and, after 1580, Newfoundland fishery and Caribbean privateering. The political obstacles to encroaching on Portuguese or Spanish preserves faded with the cooling of relations with their rulers, and there was a growing confidence in maritime power to defend extended trade. The difficulties of the old-established Antwerp trade led men to look for new ways to employ their resources—though in the 1580s and 1590s investfent in privateering seemed as good a way as any to fill warehouses with southern and Asian goods. Attempts to find a north-west passage to Asia inevitably failed, but they reinforced the interest in North America that fishing and privateering created, and the issue of this, in time,

[5] See Tables IV and V, pages 55, 56 below.

32

was colonisation in Virginia and New England. Dutch as well as English failures at the north-west and north-east passages led both to make new attempts on the Cape route to the Indian Ocean. The English East India Company was able to begin trading in the Indian Ocean in 1601 only four years behind the Dutch. Trading and colonisation enterprises began on a very modest scale in the first decade of the new century, but were soon expanded. The East India trade received a huge accession of resources (as, to a lesser extent, did the Levant trade) in the years 1615–17, when the great London merchants of the Merchants Adventurers Company, withdrawing temporarily from their regular activities as these were disrupted by the Cockayne project, poured great funds into Asian trade and permanently enlarged its scale. On the other side of the world, two factors gave American colonisation a strong new impetus after early years of weakness. The discovery in 1614–16 that Virginia could produce crops of tobacco that sold readily in Europe made Virginia settlement and the financing of it attractive. Persecution in England—above all of the Puritans in the 1630s, but also of royalists at the end of the 1640s—drove great numbers of people to emigrate to New England and the West Indies. Though both the eastward and the westward movements had the same remote origins in the desire to establish contact with the riches of Asia, any possibility of America being an intermediary trading colony disappeared once the English East India trade had been established. English enterprise in Asia and America, therefore, took entirely different forms:

In Asia, the English were no more than traders, in posts established by leave of the local territorial rulers (though some, like Bombay and Surat, came to be English-governed). Excluded by the Dutch from the Spice Islands that produced the sought-after cloves and nutmegs, their principal trading commodity was the pepper of northern Sumatra and southern India. English demand for pepper, however, was far too small to maintain Indian Ocean shipping and an eastern establishment on a scale that would give credibility to its staying power in the eyes of eastern rulers, and hold off the Dutch and the Portuguese. To carry on a trade that would support its eastern position the Company had to import pepper on a scale that could only be disposed of by large re-export. From its earliest years, it was selling pepper in northern Europe, and before 1620 in the Mediterranean as well; in the 1640s, it even shipped some to Alexandria, the Levant port from which it had once been brought to England. But the pepper market was a rather inelastic one, and though some old markets might be seized from the Portuguese, saleable new commodities had to be identified if eastern trade was to be expanded. Before the Civil War, useful contributions were made by indigo, a valuable dye for the cloth industry, and saltpetre, a bulk commodity that filled up the ship's holds. But the big growth of the trade took place when a new consumer demand in Europe was tapped by the import of cheap Indian textiles—above all, calicoes. They were brought in modest quantities, chiefly from Gujerat, before the Civil War, but it was in the second half of the century that they leaped into popular favour. By 1700 they accounted for two-thirds of the East India Company's imports. and the market for them appeared insatiable in England and in European countries to which they were re-exported. Produced in India by very low-cost labour, they could bear the cost of a ten-thousand-mile voyage and remain cheap in relation to European textiles; and, above all, they made a fresh and attractive new offering to the growing European taste for lighter materials. By the end of the century the general alarm felt by European industries caused restrictions and prohibitions to be placed on their import. In England they were specially feared for their inroads into the markets of the recently developed New Draperies, and the sale of some varieties was prohibited in 1701. This halted the growth of legally recorded imports for a time, and East India trade was stabilised after a phase of very rapid growth. Exports played very little part in East India trade; the Company sent out what goods it could hope to sell, and paid with silver for most of the imports which, sold at the auctions in London, would yield its main profits.

English trade with America, on the other hand, rested almost entirely on English colonisation; the one significant exception was Brazil, to which there was some traffic in the middle decades of the seventeenth century. The expansive element in Indian trade was a commodity almost unknown in Europe, cheap cotton cloth. America also offered a new cheap commodity, tobacco, and it greatly cheapened sugar that had once been a luxury product of Mediterranean lands. The earliest colony, Virginia, began to export tobacco in 1614; the West Indian colonies established in the twenties and early thirties followed its example. Nevertheless, the value of American trade was small before the Civil War. The tobacco trade was almost negligible in value (the official figures enormously exaggerate the trade by their over-pricing of tobacco), and the northern colonies that clustered around Massachusetts after 1629 sent only a few furs and some timber to Europe. The potentialities of American trade were already recognised. As early as 1624 an Order in Council attempted to exclude the Dutch from it, and the Navigation Acts of 1651 and 1660 were directed, with much greater success, to the same objective. During the obscure two decades of the Civil War and Interregnum, the colonial trade leaped suddenly from triviality into great importance; the statistics that became available in the early sixties show the colonies supplying an eighth of London's imports, with the total rising very rapidly year by year. Sugar then accounted for over 60% and tobacco for 17% of the total.

At the beginning of the seventeenth century, tiny quantities of expensive tobacco were imported from the Spanish Caribbean. The introduction of Trinidad plants to Virginia enabled the colony to produce saleable tobacco; production expanded rapidly and, in the course of the 1620s, the price was brought down from several shillings to a few pence a pound, while the addition of British West Indies production in the following years resulted in the price falling as low as a penny a pound. The islands turned to other products, such as cotton and ginger, but Virginia could not adopt these alternatives. Its output continued to grow rapidly, and as the new smoking habit took hold more widely in Europe, the price recovered a little, and Virginia and Maryland were again able to sell their output for a good return. Between 1615 and 1700 the English tobacco import rose from 50 thousand to 38 million pounds. At the latter date almost two-thirds of the total was exported, although a great production of tobacco had been developed in Holland and northern Germany. Cheap tobacco, like cheap eastern textiles, was irresistible; a new fashion was created, spreading down through all social classes, despite the opposition from time to time of governments concerned with public health, cleanliness or the balance of payments.

Yet tobacco was already overshadowed by sugar. England's

small imports of sugar had been supplied from Portugal during the early seventeenth century. Their source was Brazil, where production was being extended and cheapened, and when war between the Dutch and Portuguese for the Brazilian plantations caused sugar prices to rise to very high levels in the 1640s, English colonists in Barbados seized the opportunity to turn land to sugar production and make large profits. Their example was followed more slowly in other islands, and by the time peace returned to Brazil, sugar planting was firmly established in the British West Indies. They produced more cheaply than Brazil and, in the course of the 1660s, captured the northern European market from the Portuguese. By 1700 half the English import was being re-exported to Europe. This sugar market, too, was expanding under the influence of rapidly falling prices and the increasing use of fresh and dried fruits and the drinking of coffee.

During the second half of the seventeenth century, therefore, the composition of English import trade underwent great changes. Comparisons over a long period can only be made for London—but four-fifths of seventeenth-century imports came through London. Holland and Germany continued to be great suppliers of their own manufactures to England, because the German and Dutch linen industries were able to meet one aspect of the demand for variety in textiles. Comparisons are hazardous because of uncertainty about valuations, but imports of linens and mixed fabrics may have doubled in the second half of the seventeenth century, and, at its end, they constituted almost the whole of English imports from Germany and the Netherlands. The entrepôt role of Hamburg and Amsterdam almost disappeared. Trade with the Baltic and Scandinavia was expanded to serve essential English needs; and with the Mediterranean in exchange for great and growing quantities of English woollens sent to Spain, Portugal and Turkey. Above all, trade beyond the oceans grew; imports from Asia and America rose from nothing before 1600 and no more than 7% of the total in 1621, to 34% in 1700. England supplied Europe with sugar, tobacco and oriental textiles because, on the one hand, the Dutch had more interest in Indonesia than India, so that English traders operated without hindrance in the latter place; and on the other, because the Dutch, relying on their commercial superiority to give them control of colonial trades, were driven from them by English laws—

the Navigation Acts—maintained by an English political power which the Dutch could not successfully challenge. With Dutch rivalry contained in this way, and French colonial enterprise held back by France's internal troubles in the mid-century decades, England became a great entrepôt. Associated with the changing import trade, therefore, a change came over English exports too. After many centuries during which they had included little but wool and woollen goods, these were now rivalled in value by re-exported calicoes, silks, tobacco and sugar.[6]

Despite the growth of the re-export trade, woollens accounted for just half of the total of English exports in 1700. The continuing growth in their export was due principally to the continuing penetration, in ever greater depth, of the markets of southern Europe. To meet this demand, many branches of the cloth industry that had made the coarser types of cloth turned their energies to the New Draperies during the seventeenth century. Devon and Dorset frieze manufacture gave way, in the second half of the century, to the concentrated Devon manufacture of serges and perpetuanas using Irish wool. The big Norwich stuff-making industry grew up on the remains of an old and declining worsted production known as russell weaving; alongside this the Suffolk broadcloth industry, declining in the middle decades of the seventeenth century, was replaced to some extent by bay-making, though a part of its spinning capacity was turned to supplying the stuff-makers of the Norwich area. By 1700 all the leading areas that had produced cheap woollens, except the Leeds–Huddersfield area of Yorkshire, had gone over to worsteds or mixed fabrics. Yorkshire manufacturers of kerseys and dozens remained prosperous, however, exporting growing quantities of them, and, by 1700, adding some cheap varieties of broadcloth to their production. But long before this date, a worsted manufacture was springing up in the western part of the Yorkshire region around Halifax, first making bays but rapidly widening its range.

Yet the fine broadcloth making of Wiltshire and Gloucester, whose markets had been hit so early and so heavily by Dutch competition, was stable and flourishing at the end of the century and still had a large export trade. The continuance of the name 'broadcloths' for these west-country products obscures great

[6] For imports and exports c. 1700, see Table V, page 56 below.

changes in the nature of the finest cloths, which made them acceptable in new conditions. In the first place, surprisingly, high quality Spanish wool was brought in. Historians have not yet dealt adequately with this phenomenon. For the present, we can only note that the movement of the main centres of sheep rearing from poor uplands to enclosed mixed farms in England is said to have produced a lengthening and coarsening of the wool making it suitable for worsteds; while the movement of flocks from migratory life over poor uplands to living on enclosed farms in Spain was associated with a shortening and refining of their wool that made them suitable for fine woollen cloth. Wiltshire clothmakers were certainly experimenting with Spanish wool as early as the 1580s, and from the peace of 1604 onward it was increasingly used to make particular good quality cloth, which was called 'Spanish cloth' and exported to the central European market. It was very much lighter than the old broadcloth, the common weight of 23 ounces to the yard of the sixteenth century coming down to 16–18 ounces before the Civil War; and after the war, cloths weighing as little as 11 ounces to the yard were being made. So great was the change that in 1667 there is a reference to the 'broad woollen cloth of the New Draperies commonly called Spanish cloth'; an important part of the 'Old Draperies' had approached the lightness of the New, whilst retaining its essential woollen quality. In the latter part of the century, the use of the special appellation of 'Spanish cloth' ceased, as the main bulk of Wiltshire production came to be assimilated to this type, some of it still using Spanish wool.

Some of the early imports of Spanish wool or yarn may have been already dyed, and dyeing was commenced in the west of England early in the seventeenth century. This accounts for the beginning of an export of dyed west-country broadcloths in the 1620s, but it was on a small scale until dyeing and finishing to continental standards were perfected in London. By the time of the Civil War, retained imports of indigo, cochineal and Brazil wood for dyeing had reached a high level, and about a third of all broadcloths that went out in 1640 were dressed and dyed. Thereafter, the proportion rose rapidly to some two-thirds in the 1660s, and by the end of the century only a very small export of undressed white broadcloths to Holland remained. The decline in the number of cloths exported in the course of the century was counterbalanced in value by the gradual change from undyed to the much more valuable finished products.

While broadcloth export, after heavy loss of markets, eventually stabilised at a lower level, the sale of New Draperies was spreading into Holland and Germany and, through them, to central Europe in the middle decades of the century. In the south, English goods had broken into the markets of declining industries. In central and northern Europe the expansion of New Draperies had to make its way in face of competition from the longer-established and still vigorous Low Countries industries. The enormous increase in the sale of English perpetuanos and serges in Holland from the 1660s onward, that made Devon for some decades one of the greatest English industrial areas, was the counterpart not only of the collapse of sales of Hampshire kerseys and Devon friezes, but also of a steep decline in Dutch output of worsteds. Meanwhile, the Dutch broadcloth industry at Leyden was encroaching on the markets that Wiltshire and Gloucester served. This complicated interchange of markets, the growth of regional specialisations competing across both internal and international boundaries, cannot be fully explained by writers on trade. It depended on industrial situations, on changing raw material availability, labour costs, and capacity to react swiftly to changing fashion demands which were now working increasingly rapidly. By 1700 the total sale of English cloth in northern and central Europe was much the same as it had been before the Civil War, but more than half of it was now of New Draperies.

It has already been observed that new industries were founded in England in the decades around 1600 and others widened in their technical range. The Huguenot immigration of the 1680s brought a further broadening of English industry, silk and paper in particular reaching the standards of continental manufactures. England was becoming, industrially, almost self-sufficient except in linen wares. None of these newer industries, however (unless coal mining is included), was able to sell its products in a Europe that was generally at the same level of technology and industrial organisation. But there was a new colonial market, secured by the human connection between Englishmen in England and America, by the difficulty of establishing industry in America's free-land, high-wage societies, and by the obstacles, modest as they were, placed by the Navigation Acts on the sending of foreign manufactures. The colonial market was provided with woollens by local household industry and with linens largely by continental goods shipped through England; but nearly all its other manufactured needs were met by English industries, many of them only recently developed, that had hitherto produced only for home consumption. The only large industries anywhere were the textile manufactures, and the total demand for other goods from the colonies, with their mere 300,000 people in 1700, was small. But such as they were, colonial needs for silks and cottons, hats and gloves, soap, axes, knives, nails and saws and a host of other things, were met from England. These colonial sales already had a real significance for some small industries and were to develop into a huge export trade with the colonies in the eighteenth century, accounting for the third phase of rapid expansion of England's export trade.

6 Trade Organisations and Institutions

THIS study has tried to show how and why the volume, commodity structure and geographical spread of trade changed over two centuries. Basing itself on statistics, good and bad, and examining the causes of the developments they reveal, it follows the example and draws on the work of most historians who have written on the subject during the past thirty years and more. The signpost that most clearly marked the turn away from earlier lines of approach to the subject was F. J. Fisher's article, 'Commercial Trends and Policy in Sixteenth century England' in the *Economic History Review* Vol. X (1940), although some older work had foreshadowed it. Most older works were written in terms of the organisation of merchant companies rather than of actual trade and traders. Few of these companies were trading organisations; they had secondary functions as organisations to which traders in particular areas had to belong, which imposed restrictions of some kind on the activities of members and non-members. But they were conspicuous institutions in their day, and had real importance in relation to governments at home and abroad. The organisation of trade, and the part they played in some areas of it, require some consideration here.

Most trade was carried on by individuals and small partnerships, and not by the Company of Merchants Adventurers, the Levant Company (during most of its life), the Eastland Company or others of their kind. Even partnership was very limited. There were no large partnerships, for English law made no concessions in the matter of partnership responsibilities. No partner, however small his stake in terms of capital invested or share of profits, could escape legal liability, to the extent of all his personal possessions, for the debts of any partnership of which he was a member. Partnership was therefore almost confined to people who intended to take their full shares in the management of affairs, so that risks would be taken only with their positive

41

and informed consent. Evidence of genuine sleeping partnerships is rare, except when there were the closest family ties.

Though many traders in England were foreigners, all of them came completely under English law, except the German Hanseatic merchants who retained their medieval privileges until 1560. These privileges were the last obsolete remnants of the ancient organisation of trade, when England had been a country in which foreign merchants settled to buy and send away goods, bringing their own to sell. The medieval trade by sea with Italy had been entirely in Italian hands; in its closing years, English merchants were taking a growing share, but the overland traffic to Italy, that replaced it in the mid-sixteenth century, was largely carried on by Italian merchant houses operating in London. After this declined in the 1570s, Italian trades soon ceased to be important in England. Before 1500 most of the trade with Spain was in the hands of Spanish merchants settled in London and Bristol, but English traders took it over in the following decades. In the trade between London and Antwerp, foreigners normally sent out some 40% of the exported cloth, and in the 1540s their share was sometimes over a half, while their share in import trade was usually a good deal larger. Part of this was Italian, as has been seen. Another part, the size of which cannot be closely estimated, was 'Flemish' (this term, in popular usage, then embraced all Netherlands citizens), for merchants of Antwerp had their agents or partners in London, just as English merchants had them in Antwerp. The largest foreign share, fluctuating around a quarter of all exports, was that of the Hanseatic merchants. Their trade had originally been with the Baltic and Scandinavian countries, from which they still brought bulky goods by sea, but they increasingly engaged in the London–Antwerp trade in competition with English merchants, sending English goods on from Antwerp to Cologne, and northward to the towns of the Baltic hinterland. Their small privileges in England were established by long-standing treaties, and this made the task of dislodging them a painful one that raised political difficulties. As English resources in capital and commercial skill and overseas connections grew, whittling away the genuine commercial advantages the Hanseatics had once had, they were all the more anxious to cling to their treaty privileges. Nevertheless, their share of English trade fell rapidly during the second half of the century, and their protests and occasional boycotts, when privileges were reduced, did not help them—though, as we have seen, they were able to make difficulties for English merchants in Germany. By the early years of the seventeenth century, they carried on no more than three or four per cent of English trade. The role of other foreigners had become blurred by the permanent settlement of large numbers of refugee merchants, who traded on a big scale with their relations who had similarly migrated from the Netherlands to Hamburg, Leghorn or Stockholm.

A few branches of trade were carried on by joint-stock companies, in which numbers of people pooled their capital to be put under a single management. These companies, all of them chartered by the crown, were created to face special situations whose risks were too great to be supported by the capital of one or two people. All involved trading beyond Europe, at the end of long voyages, and in countries where the limited diplomatic courtesies of Europe were unknown. The earliest two of them—the Russia Company of 1555 and the Levant Company of 1581—both abandoned the joint-stock and became associations of individuals trading privately, once the trades were well-established. The Royal African Company of 1672, formed to carry on the slave trade, had to give way to private trade in 1698. Only the little Hudson's Bay Company of 1670 never wavered from joint-stock management. Individual trade, regulated or not, was the norm, and among all the joint-stock companies only the East India Company ever made a large contribution to the total of English overseas trade. The attempt, after 1698, to replace it by a company that simply regulated the operations of private traders collapsed in 1709, because the Indian Ocean trade really was a special case. The capital required was so huge that it could not be mustered except by a joint-stock company. Differing from all other trades beyond Europe in dealing with advanced civilisations, highly organised kingdoms, and Dutch competition of a political as well as a commercial kind, it had to equip itself with some of the weapons and machinery of state in order to trade with success.

There was another, older kind of organisation. named by modern historians the 'regulated' company. Regulated companies existed to cover most areas of English trade in their sixteenth century heyday, but they found no effective role in the areas of

43

seventeenth century trade expansion in southern Europe and America. They had risen to importance in the later middle ages, when their most famous and influential examples were the Company of Merchants of the Staple, set up with a monopoly of the trade in wool, and the Company of Merchants Adventurers of England, dominated by its London membership, that held a legal monopoly of Englishmen's export of woollen cloth and certain other goods to the Antwerp region. These companies were the counterparts in overseas trade of the medieval town gilds. In the absence of well-enforced and ascertainable commercial law, and of secure support by governments for their subjects who ventured abroad, merchants had once found it desirable to group together and negotiate their status with governments—national, provincial or local—and in return to give joint guarantees of their own good behaviour. Such groups, quickly realising their bargaining strength, used it to obtain further small privileges in their places of settlement overseas, as the Hansards had done in England. The English crown, anxious to have some oversight of its subjects abroad, and a channel to bring pressure on merchant communities at home, encouraged organisations of this kind and gave them charters and monopoly rights to trade in particular areas.

Such companies were becoming anachronistic in the seventeenth century. The Merchants Adventurers Company remained powerful because it contained the wealthiest English merchants, who had the ear of government and who saw an interest in restricting the entry of English traders to their territory. The new regulated companies of the 1570s and 1580s—of which only the Eastland Company, formed with a monopoly of Baltic trade, had any lasting importance—were created in the pattern of the Merchants Adventurers to secure some monopoly advantage to their members; indeed, it has been argued that they were formed because of the desire of some of the Merchants Adventurers to get into and consolidate some hold over trades pioneered by others, when the Antwerp trade was crumbling. As the Merchants Adventurers trade declined after 1614—for reasons having little connection with the existence of the Company—so did its prestige, and with it the prestige of this form of organisation. Its monopoly position was abolished from 1621 to 1634, was ambiguous during the Interregnum, and was ended for ever in 1689. The Eastland Company, created to trade with the Danzig area, became more and more irrelevant as the Baltic trade increasingly used other ports, and after 1673 it was compelled to admit anyone who applied for membership. The Russia Company was opened up in the same way in 1698. Only the Levant Company survived the century with its monopoly unbroken, because, until the 1680s, it was concerned with a fast-growing trade that had plenty of room to accept newcomers.

Much argument has been devoted to the question whether regulated companies promoted or hindered the expansion of English trade. Careful studies of the Merchants Adventurers Company of the early seventeenth century, and the Levant Company of the early eighteenth century, point strongly to the conclusion that they had very little influence either way. Trade was carried on by traders who had to learn the methods of particular branches of trade. If they did so, it was usually because they had connections among merchants, of a kind that would serve to secure their admittance of the companies. Only in the period of extreme concentration on Antwerp and the London merchants' drive to secure a dominant position in this trade did the Merchants Adventurers Company possibly have a much stronger influence on the course of events. Ex. TRADE. 1979.

Finally, we must consider how the actions of government affected overseas trade. Two kinds of government behaviour must be distinguished. One was the implementation of financial or strategic measures, or the personal whims of monarchs; that is, behaviour not primarily directed to economic ends. The other was the formulation and execution of action that did have overt economic purposes. It was taken for granted, until the end of the eighteenth century, that the government ought to intervene in economic affairs for the public good, whether in the general interest or in that of particular groups who might appeal to it. But it is not necessary to assume that there was any consistent economic policy; government interventions did not follow long-term plans with theoretical bases, but were, almost invariably, responses to the immediate problems of a particular year or month. Sometimes the resulting measures were forgotten or reversed when the immediate difficulty was over or the ineffectiveness of the action had become plain; occasionally they were built upon by similar measures and hardened in this way to have the effect of continuing policy.

The existence of a revenue tariff on imports and exports was old-established and taken for granted. Until 1689 it was extremely difficult to make important changes in it, because this revenue was involved with the delicate questions of financial control on which rested the balance between royal and parliamentary power. From 1558 until 1660 there was a step-by-step adjustment of the tariff valuations upon which duties were charged, to take account of the general price rise; there were two big steps with parliamentary approval in 1558 and 1604, a number of small ones between 1604 and the Civil War, and a final revaluation in 1660. Nevertheless, the level of tariffs was always very low (except on the consumer luxuries of wine, brandy and tobacco), and their burden on trade probably declined during the sixteenth century and was not restored. Under William III, when parliament had become sufficiently confident of its control of the purse-strings to initiate a rapid increase in tariffs, the first steps were taken that were to transform the tariff structure in the eighteenth century. The tariffs that did significantly influence the direction of late seventeenth century trade were those imposed at prohibitive rates on foreign sugar and tobacco, to reserve the English market for colonial products.

Defence needs weighed heavily with the government in bringing in the Navigation Acts, but the motives here were mixed, and will be considered below. Beyond this, personal acts of the crown to please and reward courtiers probably had greater effects on trade, up to the time of the Civil War, than considered measures of government. The open licence that Elizabeth I granted to the Earl of Cumberland to export undyed and undressed cloths in breach of the law, the Cockayne project that has been discussed, and the Courteen project that created chaos in the East India trade under Charles I, are the most evident examples, but small ones could be multiplied. After 1660, this kind of royal action ceased to be important.

In turning to explicitly economic measures, we must again look briefly at the regulated companies. From the government's point of view, one of the virtues of company organisation was that it provided channels for the transmission of government pressures. Through the Merchants Adventurers Company, at one time or another, merchants were ordered to buy cloth from the west country even if they could not sell it, to use the proceeds of their overseas sales to provide the crown's needs for foreign currency, and to send their goods in ships sailing in convoy. If the Company's rulers were recalcitrant, or their members would not submit themselves to the crown's will, the Company could be threatened with the withdrawal of its monopoly privileges—a threat that was implemented, in the case of the Merchants Adventurers, in 1621 and 1624. Until the Civil War, in fact, direct administrative action of this kind was commonplace, while, on the other hand, company organisation gave trading interests an effective means of bringing their grievances to the ear of government and asking for administrative remedies. After the Civil War, this situation too had changed; trading companies dependent on royal charters were now less confident in their status, while the accession of governmental efficiency inherited from the Cromwellian Protectorate made possible the enactment and determined enforcement of legislation.

Of course there had always been some legislation in response to the problems arising from foreign trade; for example, the spate of measures in and around 1555 to restrict the extension of the cloth industry stemmed from the decline of trade after the mid-century boom years, and was aimed at preventing future collapses by restricting the impact on industry of future booms. After the Civil War, however, there was a growth in the number of measures that had a real impact on trade. The outcries of landowners and graziers at their sufferings from Irish competition brought about the prohibition of the import of Irish cattle in 1663, and of their products—butter, cheese and so on—in 1669. This stopped the principal Irish export to England, and caused the Irish to seek new export commodities which they found first in wool, presently in woollen and linen yarn and ultimately in linen cloth. In the 1670s there was a wave of demands for action against France, which drew much of its force from political hostility, but also had an economic basis. The new government of Louis XIV, determined to build up a French woollen industry, set out to cut imports of woollen goods by steep tariff increases in 1664, 1667 and 1673. Tariff retaliation was impossible in England because of the uncertain effect on royal revenue, and the response was a prohibition, in 1678, of all imports from France. This trade embargo lasted from 1678 to 1685, and was followed by the imposition of nearly prohibitive duties on French goods from 1690.

47

The French trade, which had once been very large, was nearly strangled, and behind this protection a number of new industries grew up in England producing goods that had previously been imported.

But the Navigation Acts constitute the best-known body of commercial legislation. They arose from fear of the growing commercial and maritime power of the Dutch. The government was anxious to see a large merchant fleet that would provide seamen and auxiliary warships for the navy in wartime; merchants and shipowners wanted to prevent the Dutch taking the profits of an intermediary trade at their expense, and to preserve the English carrying trade from falling into Dutch hands just when the opportunities for its expansion were emerging. Dutch competition in the carrying trade, and the growth of the Dutch entrepôt, were countered by a series of Orders in Council from 1615 onward that attempted to confine the carriage of Baltic and Mediterranean goods to England, and all colonial trade, to English ships. Dutch competition was dampened by their involvement in the Thirty Years' War, but when it reappeared with enhanced vigour in 1648, it was quickly met by the comprehensive Commonwealth Navigation Ordinance of 1651, which pulled the earlier measures together, and this was confirmed and refined by the Navigation Act of 1660, which, with some modifications, remained in force for nearly two centuries. These were important measures for their time. Traffic with distant ports was secured to English ships, and the large merchant fleet that the government desired sprang into being. The more significant long-term result was in ensuring that the trading connections bridging the Atlantic were built up between colonial and English merchants, and that in practice, therefore, the growing needs of the colonies would be met mainly by English producers. No doubt English trade and shipping would have grown in the course of time without this legislation, but the Acts prevented English expansion in America from bringing about an increased carrying trade by Dutch vessels or the creation of a yet greater entrepôt trade at Amsterdam.

None of these acts was exclusively concerned with trade. The Irish Cattle Acts were passed in the interests of landowners, and they damaged Anglo-Irish trade. The French prohibition, so far as it had economic reasons, was one that cut off trade as a retaliation for the reduction of English exports by French action. The

Navigation Acts were closely connected with the maritime defence of the country. Yet the pattern of trade at the end of the seventeenth country, modified by these acts, was very different from what it would have been if left untrammelled.

Finally, governments had a powerful influence on trade by entering into wars, and occasionally into intense quarrels that stopped short of war. This is a subject that economic historians tend to avoid, for war involves interruption of the working of natural economic forces. But war was not exceptional; England was engaged in external wars during some seventy of these two hundred years, often with its major trading partners, the Spanish rulers of the Netherlands in the sixteenth century and the Dutch in the seventeenth. Seizures of goods, losses of ships, the abandonment of some trade routes and the diversion of others, characterised these wars. When England was not at war itself, it suffered (or, very occasionally, benefited) from the wars of others—for example, the Schmalkaldic Wars, the Dutch War of Independence and the Thirty Years' War. Overseas trade was particularly susceptible to disturbance by war; the astonishing thing, surveying this long period of history, is how resilient it was in recovering instantly when their pressure was lifted. But the short-term fluctuations in trade, on which war was the most powerful influence, cannot be examined in this study, which has set out to explain the long-term movements over two centuries.

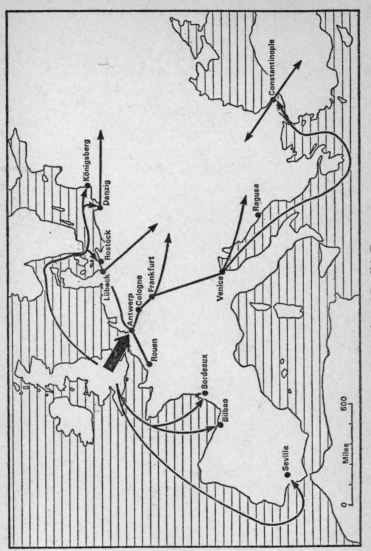

Destination of English Exports, 1500

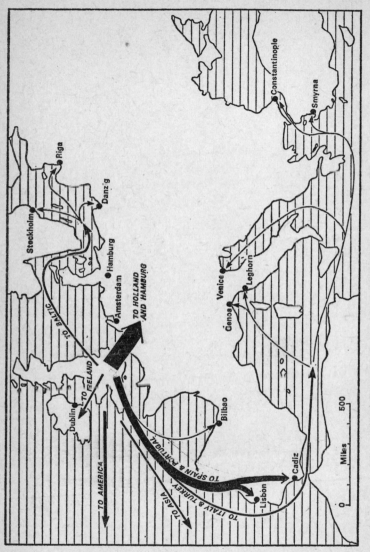

Destination of English Exports, 1700

Riga

Danz'g

Steckholm

Hamburg

Amsterdam

Constantinople

Smyrna

Venice

Leghorn

Genoa

TO BALTIC

TO HOLLAND
AND HAMBURG

TO IRELAND

Dublin

Bilbao

TO SPAIN & PORTUGAL

Cadiz

Lisbon

TO ITALY & TURKEY

TO ASIA

TO AMERICA

0

500

Miles

TABLE I

Number of cloths exported from London and provincial ports, 1473–1561
(thousands of notional shortcloths)

	Total	London	Outports
1473–7	37	29	8
1478–82	59	40	19
1483–7	44	32	12
1488–92	53	38	15
1493–7		n.a.*	
1498–1502	69	46	23
1503–7	75	46	29
1508–12	84	57	27
1513–17	88	61	27
1518–22	84	62	22
1523–7	91	69	22
1528–32	91	70	21
1533–7	102	85	17
1538–42	116	98	18
1543–7	126	112	14
1550–2	126	110	(16)†
1559–61	118	104	(14)

* n.a.—not available.
† Totals in parentheses are estimates from incomplete figures.

Sources: Carus-Wilson, E. M. and Coleman, O. (eds.), *England's Export Trade, 1275–1547* (1963); Fisher, F. J., 'Commercial Trends and Policy in Sixteenth Century England', *Economic History Review*, 1st series X (1940); Stone, L., 'State Control in Sixteenth-Century England', *Economic History Review*, 1st series, XVII (1947); Gould, J. D., *The Great Debasement: Currency and the Economy in mid-Tudor England* (1970). From 1559 onward, 11% has been added to the figures presented by these authorities, to allow for cloth sent as wrappers (see p. 17 *supra*).

The Customs authorities had a formula for equating each type of cloth to the worth of a shortcloth, e.g. 3 northern kerseys or 4 Devon dozens = one shortcloth. (See Tawney, R. H. and Power, E., *Tudor Economic Documents*, Vol. I, 1924, pp. 218–19.) The above figures are in 'notional shortcloths' so calculated.

TABLE II

Number of cloths exported from London, 1562–1669 (thousands of notional shortcloths) *and total value of certain other exports from London, 1598–1669*

(thousands of £s)

	Shortcloths		Official value of other goods exported
1562–4	68		
1565–7	106		
1568–70	104		
1571–3	81		
1574–6	111		
1577–9	109		
1580–2	109		
1583–5	112		
1586–8	106		
1589–91	110		
1592–4	113		
1598–1600	114		£119
1601–3	116		£130
1604	125		
1612			£356
1614	(144)*		
1620	(95)		
1640	96		£695
1663	79	(£576)	£1465
1669	85	(£684)	£1372

* Totals in parentheses are estimates from incomplete figures.

Sources: Fisher, F. J., 'Commercial Trends and Policy in Sixteenth Century England', *Economic History Review*, 1st series, X (1940); Fisher, F. J., 'London's Export Trade in the Early Seventeenth Century', *Economic History Review*, 2nd series, III (1950); BM Add. MS. 36785.

TABLE III

Exports of Old Draperies, early seventeenth century

(thousands of cloths)

(a) *London* exports by Englishmen

Notional shortcloths	126
Actual cloths of various main types: (approximate numbers)	
Western broadcloths	96 (76 undressed) to Germany and Netherlands
Suffolk cloths	15 (two-thirds to Baltic and Russia, most of the rest to Mediterranean)
Northern kerseys	23 (France and Mediterranean)
Hampshire and Devon kerseys	11 (Mediterranean)

(b) *Provincial* exports (various years between 1609 and 1624)

(i) North-east ports, Newcastle to Hull

Notional shortcloths	24
Actual cloths:	
northern kerseys	60 (three-quarters to Baltic,
northern dozens	7 one-quarter to Germany and Netherlands)

(ii) East Anglian ports, Lynn to Colchester

Notional shortcloths	5 (nearly all Suffolk cloths, to Baltic)

(iii) Southern ports, Dover to Exeter

Notional shortcloths	21
Actual cloths:	
Berks and Dorset kerseys	42 Devon and Dorset dozens, 15 Devon (nearly all to France, some to Spain)

(iv) Western ports, Barnstaple to Chester

Notional shortcloths	1 (to France and Spain)

Source: Friis, A., *Alderman Cockayne's Project and the Cloth Trade* (1927). With all its drawbacks, this table gives a good notion of the distribution of the trade. No adjustment has been made for wrappers. Alien exports from London are not likely to have exceeded 5 thousand notional shortcloths.

TABLE IV

London Imports, 1621, average of 1663 and 1669, and average of 1699–1701

(thousands of £s)

	Europe, north of Alps and Pyrenees			Southern Europe and Turkey			America and Asia			TOTAL		
	1621	1660s	1700	1621	1660s	1700	1621	1660s	1700	1621	1660s	1700
Textiles	407	804	837	19	105	83	—	211	474	426	1120	1394
Other manufactures	36	151	139	—	17	26	—	4	78	36	172	213
Wine and Brandy	146	64	41	134	80	426	—	—	—	280	144	467
Sugar	—	—	—	83	36	—	—	256	526	83	292	526
Tobacco	16	—	—	33	1	—	14	69	161	63	70	161
Fruit	7	3	6	68	193	129	—	—	—	75	196	135
Pepper	10	—	—	1	—	—	77	80	103	88	80	103
Other foodstuffs	73	84	48	12	31	76	—	48	67	90	163	191
Silk	94	—	1	45	262	301	4	1	42	143	263	344
Textile yarns	15	20	128	—	55	37	—	8	4	15	83	169
Dyestuffs	31	36	34	29	91	90	—	19	79	60	146	203
Other raw materials	144	418	460	69	214	216	6	134	85	219	766	761
	984	1580	1664	493	1085	1384	101	830	1619	1578	3495	4667

Sources: A. M. Millard, 'The Import Trade of London, 1600–1640' (unpublished London Ph.D. thesis, 1956); Davis, R., 'English Foreign Trade, 1660–1700', *Economic History Review*, VII (1954).

TABLE V

English Foreign Trade, average of years 1699–1701
(thousands of £s)

	Europe north of Alps and Pyrenees	*Southern Europe and Turkey*	*America and Asia*	*TOTAL*
EXPORTS				
woollens	1570	1201	274	3045
other mfrs.	153	73	312	538
foodstuffs	303	128	57	488
raw materials	262	82	18	362
TOTAL	2288	1484	661	4433
Re-exports	1436	224	326	1986
TOTAL EXPORTS	3724	1708	987	6419
IMPORTS				
textiles	1000	83	474	1557
other mfrs.	181	28	78	287
foodstuffs	163	747	1059	1969
raw materials	1087	697	252	2036
TOTAL IMPORTS	2431	1555	1863	5849

Source: Davis, R., 'English Foreign Trade, 1660–1700', *Economic History Review*, 2nd series, VII (1954).

Select Bibliography

K. R. Andrews, *Elizabethan Privateering* (1964). A discussion of its economic aspects, showing the role of merchant capital.

S.-E. Åström, *The Customs Accounts as Sources for the Study of Trade* (1965). A valuable detailed critique of the English records.

S.-E. Åström, *From Cloth to Iron: the Anglo-Baltic Trade in the Seventeenth Century* (1965). The best exposition of this subject.

S.-E. Åström, 'The Reliability of the English Port Brooks', *Scandinavian Economic History Review.*, XVI (1968). Makes comparisons between the trade as shown by Baltic records and the English port books, which suggest a reasonable degree of reliability.

N. Bang & K. Korst, *Tabeller over Skibsfart og Varetransport gennem Öresund, 1497-1783* (1906-45). This vast collection, summarising the records of the Danish tolls at the entrance to the Baltic, contains essential statistics on Anglo-Baltic trade.

P. J. Bowden, 'Wool Supply and the Woollen Industry', *Economic History Review*, 2nd series, IX (1956). Advances the view that the turn to manufacture of the New Draperies was made necessary by changing quality of English wool.

W. Brulez, 'Les Routes Commerciales d'Angleterre en Italie au XVI Siècle', *Studi in Onore di Amintore Fanfani,* IV (1962). Estimates the relative importance of overland routes.

E. M. Carus-Wilson & O. Coleman (eds.), *England's Export Trade, 1275-1547* (1963). The essential statistics clearly set out, with a useful introduction on their validity and significance.

K. N. Chaudhuri, *The English East India Company* (1965). An excellent discussion of the trade in its first forty years.

D. C. Coleman, 'An Innovation and its Diffusion : The New Draperies', *Economic History Review,* 2nd series, XXI (1968). Examines the continental origins of this manufacture.

D. C. Coleman (ed.), *Revisions in Mercantilism* (1969). A collection of contributions on this topic, among which the editor's own is outstanding.

G. E. Connell-Smith, *Forerunners of Drake* (1954). Despite its title, this is about Anglo-Spanish trade in the early sixteenth century.

L. M. Cullen, *Anglo-Irish Trade 1660–1800* (1968). A clear and thorough discussion of the course of trade and of business methods.

K. G. Davies, *The Royal African Company* (1957). The early history of the English slave trade.

R. Davis, 'England and the Mediterranean, 1570–1670', in F. J. Fisher (ed.), *Essays in the Economic and Social History of Tudor and Stuart England* (1961). Examines the great change that came over the pattern of trading relationships in this period.

R. Davis, 'English Foreign Trade, 1660–1700', *Economic History Review*, 2nd series, VII (1954). An analysis and commentary on the statistics.

R. Davis, *The Rise of the English Shipping Industry in the Seventeenth and Eighteenth Centuries* (1962). Considers trade from the point of view of physical quantities rather than values.

R. Davis, *The Trade and Shipping of Hull, 1500–1700* (1964). The one provincial port that retained some importance throughout the period.

B. Dietz (ed.), *The Port and Trade of Elizabethan London* (1971). A transcription of the Inward Port Book of 1567–8, with some supplementary documents and an introduction.

F. J. Fisher, 'Commercial Trends and Policy in Sixteenth century England', *Economic History Review*, 1st series X (1940). A brilliant analysis, from which modern work on the subject takes its form.

F. J. Fisher (ed.), *Sackville (Knole) Mss.*, Vol. II (Historical Manuscripts Commission, 1966). The business correspondence of Lionel Cranfield, 1597–1612, throwing a vivid light on the working of trade between England and Germany and the Netherlands.

W. Foster, *England's Quest of Eastern Trade* (1933). A good discussion of exploratory efforts and the motives behind them.

A. Friis, *Alderman Cockayne's Project and the Cloth Trade* (1927). Despite its title, this book contains the best general account of the organisation of the cloth export trade in decades before the Civil War.

J. D. Gould, *The Great Debasement: Currency and the Economy in mid-Tudor England* (1970). Contains a useful analysis of the export boom of the first half of the century, vitiated by the author's unwillingness to look beyond a limited range of data.

J. D. Gould, 'The Trade Depression of the Early 1620's', *Economic History Review*, 2nd series, VII (1954). Puts forward a different view from Supple's.

R. Gravil, 'Trading to Spain and Portugal, 1670–1700', *Business History*, X (1968). A clear account of the commodities and methods of trade.

E. F. Heckscher, 'Multilateralism, Baltic Trade and the Mercantilists', *Economic History Review*, 2nd series, III (1950). A reply to Wilson.

R. W. K. Hinton, *The Eastland Trade and the Common Weal* (1959). The seventeenth century growth of Baltic trade, with a good discussion of the repercussions in policy and economic attitudes.

W. G. Hoskins, *Industry, Trade and People in Exeter, 1688–1800* (1935). Follows Stephens into the peak and decline of the Devon serge trade.

Bal Krishna, *Commercial Relations between India and England, 1601–1757* (1924). A pioneering work in examining the actual functioning of trade, containing much useful information.

P. V. McGrath (ed.), *Merchants and Merchandise in 17th Century Bristol* (1955). A useful collection of documents.

W. E. Minchinton (ed.), *The Growth of English Overseas Trade in the Seventeenth and Eighteenth Centuries* (1969). A collection of important articles by various authors, with a useful introduction by the editor.

C. P. Nettels, 'England's Trade with New England and New York, 1685–1720', *Publications of the Colonial Society of Massachusetts*, XVIII (1935). A thorough analysis of the problems of this trade.

R. Pares, *Merchants and Planters* (1960). A brilliant exposition of the character of the English connection with the West Indies.

J. M. Price, 'Multi-Lateralism and/or Bilateralism : The Settlement of British Trade Balances with the North, c. 1700', *Economic History Review*, 2nd series, XIV (1961). The last shot in the Wilson–Heckscher–Åström controversy over the manner in which trade deficits were settled.

J. M. Price, *The Tobacco Adventure to Russia* (1961). Illuminates the whole of Anglo-Russian trade in the late seventeenth century and the composition and interests of the London merchant community.

M. Priestley, 'Anglo-French Trade and the Unfavourable Balance Controversy, 1660–1685', *Economic History Review*, 2nd series, IV (1951). The background of the embargo on trade.

G. D. Ramsay, *English Overseas Trade in the Centuries of Emergence* (1957). Much the best general survey, summarising much English and foreign work up to its time of publication.

G. D. Ramsay (ed.), *John Isham, Mercer and Merchant Adventurer* (1962). The long introduction is a first-rate account of business methods in the London–Antwerp trade of the mid-sixteenth century.

G. D. Ramsay, *The Wiltshire Woollen Industry in the Sixteenth and Seventeenth Centuries* (1942). The standard work on the principal centre of broadcloth manufacture, and its markets.

A. A. Ruddock, 'London Capitalists and the Decline of Southampton in the Early Tudor Period', *Economic History Review*, 2nd series, II (1949). Explains the transfer of Southampton's trade to London.

G. Schanz, *Englische Handelspolitik gegen Ende des Mittelalters* (1881). Contains many otherwise unpublished English documents on the trade of the early sixteenth century.

W. R. Scott, *The Constitution and Finance of English, Scottish and Irish Joint Stock Companies to 1720* (1912). Standard, and excellent, account of economic fluctuations and of the joint-stock companies in foreign trade.

V. M. Shillington & A. B. W. Chapman, *The Commercial Relations of England and Portugal* (1907). The standard work, still useful for its factual information.

O. de Smedt, *De Engelse Natie te Antwerpen in de 16ᵉ Eeuw* (1950). A thorough and detailed examination of the Merchant Adventurers and their trade, making extensive use of Dutch and German records.

W. B. Stephens, 'The Cloth Exports of the Provincial Ports, 1600–1640', *Economic History Review*, 2nd series, XXII (1969). A valuable statistical study.

W. B. Stephens, *Seventeenth Century Exeter* (1958). Shows the emergence of a great centre of 'New Draperies' out of a minor outlier of the old trade in woollens.

L. Stone, 'State Control in Sixteenth-Century England', *Economic History Review*, 1st series, XVIII (1947). A reply to Fisher's 'Commercial Trends', drawing attention particularly to the influence of political events on the course of trade.

B. E. Supple, *Commercial Crisis and Change in England, 1600–1642*

(1959). A masterly analysis of London trade fluctuations, the influences on them at home and abroad, and the response in government policy.

R. H. Tawney, *Business and Politics Under James I* (1958). The business career of Lionel Cranfield, a great merchant trading to Germany and the Netherlands.

R. H. Tawney & E. Power, *Tudor Economic Documents* (1924). Contains many documents illustrative of commerce and its relation to industry and to government policy-making.

H. W. Taylor, 'Price Revolution or Price Revision : The English and Spanish Trade After 1604', *Renaissance and Modern Studies,* XII (1968). Examines Anglo-Spanish trade and its relation to bullion supplies in the first forty years of the seventeenth century.

G. Unwin, 'The Merchant Adventurers in the Reign of Elizabeth', in R. H. Tawney (ed.), *Studies in Economic History* (1927). A strong free-trader's attack on the view that the Merchant Adventurers Company was beneficial to English trade.

J. A. Van Houtte, 'Anvers aux XV et XVI Siècles', *Annales,* XVI (1961). Much the best account of Antwerp at its peak, and the beginnings of the weakening of its economic position.

T. S. Willan, *The Early History of the Russia Company, 1555–1603* (1956). An excellent account of its organisation and trading activities.

T. S. Willan, 'Some Aspects of English Trade with the Levant in the Sixteenth Century', *English Historical Review,* LXX (1955). The best discussion of early Levant trade.

T. S. Willan, *Studies in Elizabethan Foreign Trade* (1959). Useful essays on a variety of topics, notably the Morocco trade and the role of factors.

T. S. Willan (ed.), *A Tudor Book of Rates* (1962). The introduction provides a good account of the Elizabethan customs system.

C. Wilson, 'Cloth Production and International Competition in the Seventeenth Century', *Economic History Review,* 2nd series, XIII (1960). Examines the changing roles of English and Dutch in the trades in broadcloth and worsteds.

C. Wilson, 'Treasure and Trade Balances : Further Evidence', *Economic History Review,* 2nd series, IV (1951). A reply to Heckscher.

C. Wilson, 'Treasure and Trade Balances : The Mercantilist Problem', *Economic History Review,* 2nd series, II (1949). The first shot in a controversy on the settlement of trade balances with the Baltic.

Index